The One-Person Marketing Plan™ Workbook

Third Edition

C.J. Hayden

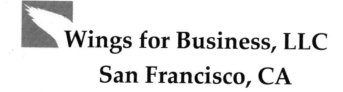

Wings for Business, LLC
San Francisco, CA

The One-Person Marketing Plan™ Workbook
Copyright © 2014 C.J. Hayden
www.getclientsnow.com

Published by Wings for Business, LLC
P.O. Box 225008 ● San Francisco, CA 94122
www.wingsforbusiness.com

ISBN-10: 0692255834
ISBN-13: 978-0692255834

*Printing/manufacturing information for this book
may be found on the last page.*

Vision without action is a daydream. Action without vision is a nightmare.
— JAPANESE PROVERB

CONTENTS

Introduction 1
   How to Use This Book 1
What Is Marketing? 3
   What Works & What Doesn't? 3
   Marketing Strategies for Professional Services 5
   59 Tactics for Marketing Your Services 6
   Marketing Tactics Guide 8
Defining Your Business Mix 15
   Business Mix Worksheet Examples 15
   Your Business Mix Worksheet 18
Choosing Where to Focus 21
   The Universal Marketing Cycle 23
   Where to Focus Your Marketing 24
   What Strategies Should You Use? 24
   Where Are You Stuck? 25
   What Should You Do? 25
   Which Strategies Will You Use? 26
Weighting Your Strategies 27
   Marketing Strategy Pie Example 28
   Your Marketing Strategy Pie 29
   Slicing the Strategy Pie 30
Selecting a Target Market 31
   Qualifying and Labeling Your Market 32
   Individual Client Profile 33
   Organizational Client Profile 34
Setting Marketing Goals 35
   Marketing Goals Worksheet Examples 36
   Your Marketing Goals Worksheet 38
Choosing a Marketing Budget 41
   Budgeting Marketing Time 41
   Marketing Hours Worksheet Example 41
   Your Marketing Hours Worksheet 42
   Budgeting Marketing Money 43
   Marketing Money Worksheet Example 43
   Your Marketing Money Worksheet 44

Defining Your Marketing Tactics 45
  Your Marketing Tactics Worksheet 46
Selecting Your Marketing Tools 47
  57 Tools for Marketing Your Services 48
  Marketing Tools Guide 50
  Your Marketing Tools Worksheet 54
Creating Your Marketing Plan 55
  Planning Your Model Month 55
  What If Your Plan Seems Impossible? 57
  From Your Model Month to a Six-Month Plan 57
  Marketing Plan Worksheet 59
  Marketing Plan Worksheet Examples 61
  Your Marketing Plan Worksheet 64
What Do You Need to Be Successful? 65
  Focus 65
  Expertise 66
  Commitment 66
  About the Author 67

INTRODUCTION

You can't just sit there and wait for people to give you that golden dream; you've got to get out there and make it happen for yourself.
— DIANA ROSS

Welcome! By opening this book, you have taken an important first step toward making your marketing more successful. If you sell your own professional services, operate a one-person service business, or you are the chief rainmaker for your firm, the One-Person Marketing Plan™ is the focused approach you need. Here are just some of the many categories of businesspeople who will benefit from using One-Person Marketing:

Accountants • Architects • Attorneys • Bodyworkers • Chiropractors
Coaches • Computer Professionals • Consultants • Counselors • Designers
Engineers • Financial Planners • Freelancers • Health Practitioners
Insurance and Investment Brokers • Photographers • Real Estate Agents
Recruiters • Speakers • Therapists • Trainers • Writers

No matter what your profession, you need a marketing plan! A marketing plan makes your marketing more effective. It enables you to focus your efforts, creates consistency in your marketing, and helps you spend your time and money wisely. In this book, you will learn about six different strategies for marketing professional services, 59 tactics and 57 tools for employing those strategies, how to choose the right tactics and tools for your unique situation, and a step-by-step process for building a powerful One-Person Marketing Plan. You will finish this book with a six-month plan you can begin using immediately to find clients, generate referrals, and close sales.

How to Use This Book

If you already own C.J. Hayden's book *Get Clients Now!*™, you will notice that some material about marketing strategies, tactics, and tools appears in both books. Including that material in both books allows each of them to stand alone. *Get Clients Now!* provides an action-oriented 28-day marketing plan, while this book outlines a detailed six-month marketing plan. This book is recommended as the "next step" after *Get Clients Now!* because the more comprehensive One-Person Marketing Plan outlined here answers several important questions *Get Clients Now!* doesn't address:

- How much marketing will it take to reach my sales and revenue goals?
- How much time and money can I afford to spend on marketing?
- How can I market for more than one line of business at the same time?
- How can I build a business model that supports my financial goals?

If you don't yet own *Get Clients Now!*, you may find that you would like additional information about the marketing strategies, tactics, and tools described in this book. If so, *Get Clients Now!* can help you, because it contains detailed "recipes" for putting your plans into action. That's why owning both books is the best combination. You can purchase a copy of *Get Clients Now!* from our website or any major bookseller.

You will get the most value from this book if you commit from the outset to complete the exercises as you go. If you're reading the PDF ebook edition, you can print extra copies of any of the worksheets from the book's Adobe Acrobat file. If you're reading the print or Kindle edition, the worksheets that don't include any calculations are simple enough for you to quickly create your own.

For the worksheets that include calculations, you may wish to use spreadsheet software to add up the variables you enter automatically. You can download Excel versions of these worksheets in the "Free Resources" section of www.getclientsnow.com.

WHAT IS MARKETING?

A goal without a plan is just a wish.
– ANTOINE DE SAINT-EXUPÉRY

To begin the process of building a powerful, effective marketing plan, let's first define what marketing is. Marketing is not rocket science; it's really very simple. **Marketing is telling people what you do... over and over.** There are many ways of telling people – in person, by phone, in writing, on the web, through the media – but you do have to *tell* them. You can't just wait for the phone to start ringing. You also have to tell them over and over. No one will remember you if they hear about you only once.

What Works & What Doesn't?

How do people in your line of work – consulting, coaching, and other professional services – get clients? Ask any successful businessperson that question and this is what you will hear: "Referrals." "Networking." "Making contacts and following up." "Word of mouth."

Look at the diagram "Marketing Strategies for Professional Services" on page 5. This diagram operates on three levels simultaneously.

First, it shows the six available sales and marketing **strategies** that service providers can use:

1. Direct Contact & Follow-Up
2. Networking & Referral Building
3. Public Speaking
4. Writing & Publicity
5. Promotional Events
6. Advertising

Second, the "Marketing Strategies" diagram rates the strategies in order of **effectiveness**, from Direct Contact at the top to Advertising at the bottom. The exact order of the individual strategies on the diagram is unimportant, but the overall effectiveness ranking is critical to making the right choices about marketing. Direct Contact and Follow-Up is an effective strategy all by itself, but Advertising, used alone, almost never works to find clients for a professional, consultant, or coach.

The effectiveness rating shown in this diagram for these strategies refers specifically to their use in marketing your own services or the services of your firm. If your business also includes product sales as part of a service package, or as an added option for existing clients, this diagram is still completely relevant to your business. However, defining appropriate marketing strategies to sell products *separately* from your services — whether in your place of business or online — is outside the scope of this book.

The third level of information shown on the diagram is the **impact** that each strategy creates: Outreach, Visibility, and/or Credibility. Knowing the impact of a strategy will help you determine how to use it. Strategies that focus on Outreach work the best, and those that focus only on Visibility are the least effective. Strategies that combine Visibility with Credibility are ranked in the middle.

Every **strategy** is made up of one or more **tactics**, or to put it another way, you use specific tactics to execute a chosen strategy. A list of the tactics you might use to execute each strategy appears on pages 6-7, and a guide to the tactics follows. (But complete the "Where to Focus Your Marketing" exercise on page 24 before you read the entire tactics guide!)

You are *not* going to use all of these tactics to build your marketing plan. You will be using only a few of these tactics at any one time. So don't allow the list of possibilities to overwhelm you; just let it inform you.

Marketing Strategies for Professional Services

59 Tactics for Marketing Your Services

Direct Contact and Follow-Up
- Cold Calling
- Warm Calling
- Lunch or Coffee (with prospects)
- In-Person or Phone Appointments
- Personal Letters and Emails
- Text Messages, Instant Messages, and Social Media "Shouts"
- Announcement Card or Letter
- Nice-to-Meet-You Notes
- Sending Articles or Links
- Extending Invitations
- Reminder Postcards or Mailers
- Newsletters and Ezines
- Broadcast Email and Autoresponders

Networking and Referral Building
- Attending Meetings and Seminars
- Developing Referral Partners
- Participating in Online Communities
- Lunch or Coffee (with contacts)
- Staying in Touch with Former Clients
- Volunteering and Serving on Committees
- Sharing Information and Resources
- Collaborations and Strategic Alliances
- Swapping Contacts
- Leads Groups
- Giving Referrals

Public Speaking
- Acting as Master of Ceremonies
- Serving on Panels
- Making Presentations
- Virtual Speaking
- Giving Classes or Workshops

59 Tactics for Marketing Your Services (*continued*)

Writing and Publicity
- Publishing Articles or Tips
- Reprinting Previously Written Articles
- Writing a Column
- Publishing a Blog
- Being Quoted by the Media
- Having Stories Published About You
- Being Interviewed on Broadcast Media
- Getting Others to Link to Your Website
- Posting to Social Media

Promotional Events
- Trade Shows
- Live Seminars, Workshops, or Demonstrations
- Virtual Seminars
- Open House or Reception
- Co-Sponsored Events
- Networking Lunch, Breakfast, or Mixer
- Giveaways, Contests, and Surveys

Advertising
- Increasing Website Visibility
- Pay-per-Click Advertising
- Online Directories
- Print Directories
- Online Classifieds
- Newspaper or Magazine Classifieds
- Banner Ads
- Print Display Ads
- Event or Conference Programs
- Unsolicited Bulk Email or Text Ads
- Direct Mail
- Brochure or Flyer Distribution
- Radio or TV Ads
- Billboards

Marketing Tactics Guide

Direct Contact and Follow-Up

1. **Cold Calling.** Call a complete stranger on the phone. Works best if you have reason to believe the person currently needs your service and you can easily explain why that is.
2. **Warm Calling.** Call prospects with whom you have some connection—people you have met before, who have been referred to you, or who belong to a professional or personal community where you are also a member.
3. **Lunch or Coffee (with prospects).** An excellent follow-up tactic when your services are expensive or difficult to explain, or the sales cycle is long.
4. **In-Person or Phone Appointments.** What many people do to hold a sales conversation to discuss their services in detail. May lead to a proposal or quote, or directly to a sale.
5. **Personal Letters and Emails.** Send a personal letter by postal mail or email to a hot prospect. Most effective when it is truly personal, not just boilerplate, and is coupled with a follow-up phone call.
6. **Text Messages, Instant Messages, and Social Media "Shouts."** Brief messages sent by text, instant message, online chat, or social media post aimed at an individual. Useful for quick hellos, reminders, or requests to prospects who are active on the platform you are using.
7. **Announcement Card or Letter.** A great way to let everyone know what you're doing if you're just getting started or have made changes in your business. Best when followed up with phone calls.
8. **Nice-to-Meet-You Notes.** When you meet someone and collect his or her business card, send a follow-up note by mail enclosing your card, or an email with your contact information.
9. **Sending Articles or Links.** Keep in touch with prospects in a nonpromotional way by mailing articles or forwarding links to websites or online posts they might find useful.
10. **Extending Invitations.** Invite prospects to a meeting or seminar you are planning to go to anyway. It's a good reason to re-contact them without doing any selling.
11. **Reminder Postcards or Mailers.** An occasional mailing reminds people what you have to offer. Postcards and self-mailers can be easier and cheaper than a print newsletter.
12. **Newsletters and Ezines.** A powerful follow-up technique when your services provide valuable information. Use print or email newsletters to show off your expertise and remind people you're available.

Marketing Tactics Guide: Direct Contact and Follow-Up (*continued*)

13. **Broadcast Email and Autoresponders.** Broadcast emails can provide prospects with additional reasons to hire you. You can set up an automated sequence of emails to follow up with prospects over time. Broadcast email should only be used when a prospect has already expressed interest in your offerings and opted in to receive your email.

Networking and Referral Building

14. **Attending Meetings and Seminars.** One of the best ways to meet people, because many of them have come for the express purpose of making new contacts. Also a good follow-up technique if you keep returning to the same group.
15. **Developing Referral Partners.** Get to know people who serve the same type of clients you do, no matter what their business is. Some professionals get most of their business from alliances with partners like these.
16. **Participating in Online Communities.** Interacting with the members of online discussion groups, message boards, chat rooms, and social networking platforms, or the readers of blogs, allows you to network without leaving your home or office.
17. **Lunch or Coffee (with contacts).** A good way to become acquainted with referral partners, colleagues, and centers of influence. Your goal is to get them to know, like, and trust you.
18. **Staying in Touch with Former Clients.** Your best source of referrals can be people who have already worked with you. Keep in touch and don't be afraid to ask them to refer others.
19. **Volunteering and Serving on Committees.** Volunteer your professional services for a high-profile nonprofit to get recognition. Serve your professional community as an officer or committee chair to gain more visibility.
20. **Sharing Information and Resources.** Pass along articles, posts, or websites of interest, invitations to events, and other ideas and opportunities to the people in your network. They will come to think of you as a resource and refer others to you.
21. **Collaborations and Strategic Alliances.** An excellent way for any small business to expand contacts and visibility. Your collaborator may know another whole circle of people.
22. **Swapping Contacts.** Exchange leads or past clients with a referral partner in a noncompetitive business. You could even send letters introducing each other.

Marketing Tactics Guide: Networking and Referral Building (*continued*)

23. **Leads Groups.** A group of people who meet regularly to exchange contacts, leads, and referrals. If you can't find one you like, start your own.
24. **Giving Referrals.** One of the best ways to get people to refer you business is to refer business to them. Always be on the lookout for opportunities to refer.

Public Speaking

25. **Acting as Master of Ceremonies.** Any excuse for standing up in front of a group will make you more visible and memorable. If you serve a group as an officer or committee chair, you'll have opportunities to make announcements or introductions.
26. **Serving on Panels.** An easy way to break into public speaking without having to prepare an entire talk. Let colleagues know you are available to speak on your area of expertise.
27. **Making Presentations.** Every meeting or conference needs speakers. Most of them are people like you, speaking for free to promote their business. It brings you visibility and credibility both.
28. **Virtual Speaking.** Many speaking opportunities exist on webinars, teleseminars, and online chats sponsored by associations, vendors, and professional schools. You can speak to an international audience without traveling.
29. **Giving Classes or Workshops.** If you really enjoy speaking or teaching, this is an effective way to expose prospective clients to your expertise. If they like you, they will want more of you.

Writing and Publicity

30. **Publishing Articles or Tips.** When you publish an article or brief tip online or in print, people not only read it and get in touch; you can also send it to your mailing list, link to it from your website or social media posts, and use it in your marketing kit.
31. **Reprinting Previously Written Articles.** Get more mileage out of each article you write by finding multiple publications and websites to publish it.
32. **Writing a Column.** When you appear regularly in the same publication or site, people who read your column will remember you and consider you as an expert.
33. **Publishing a Blog.** Making regular posts to a blog can prove your expertise, keep you in touch with prospects, and attract new people to your pipeline.

Marketing Tactics Guide: Writing and Publicity (*continued*)

34. **Being Quoted by the Media.** You can make this happen by writing to journalists, commentators, or bloggers when you see or hear your area of expertise being discussed. Next time, they may contact you for a quote or refer to your work.

35. **Having Stories Published About You.** Send a press release about your work, opinions, or achievements to editors that cover your area, or publish a release online. You can also contact a freelance writer in your field to let him or her know how interesting you are.

36. **Being Interviewed on Broadcast Media.** Pitch yourself to producers as a fascinating subject for radio, TV, or webcast interviews. Once you have appeared in just one media outlet, others will often be eager to have you as a guest.

37. **Getting Others to Link to Your Website.** Increase your web presence by letting people know about the useful content on your website via your ezine, blog, or social media posts.

38. **Posting to Social Media.** Making posts on social networking platforms can expand your visibility and credibility, once you have built a network of followers. You can post helpful tips or resources, news about your business, updates on your professional activities, or photos and videos showing your work.

Promotional Events

39. **Trade Shows.** Booths at big shows can be very expensive, but many associations put on more affordable tabletop expos. Trade shows are better for making contacts than for closing sales.

40. **Live Seminars, Workshops, or Demonstrations.** Offer a free demonstration or low-cost workshop to your existing prospect list. If you can fill the room, this can be a useful credibility booster.

41. **Virtual Seminars.** Offering a workshop via webinar – or giving a talk via teleseminar – allows you to invite prospects from around the world.

42. **Open House or Reception.** Find an excuse to throw a party, and invite prospects and referral partners. People who don't return your calls may surprise you by showing up.

43. **Co-Sponsored Events.** Co-sponsoring a workshop, symposium, or fund-raiser with a nonprofit will attract clients who support the cause. Collaborating with colleagues on an event will maximize your resources and extend your reach.

Marketing Tactics Guide: Promotional Events (*continued*)

44. **Networking Lunch, Breakfast, or Mixer.** Invite clients, prospects, and referral partners to meet each other for their own benefit. Tell everyone to bring a guest.

45. **Giveaways, Contests, and Surveys.** Offer a free gift, or a drawing for one, in return for collecting a prospect's contact information. Or conduct a survey of potential clients and offer to share the results with all participants. Be sure to target your audience carefully to avoid cluttering up your prospect list with people who will never become clients.

Advertising

46. **Increasing Website Visibility.** A website by itself is a tool rather than a tactic. You may wish to use your site primarily as an online brochure: sending visitors to it with other tactics rather than expecting it to attract traffic on its own. Or you can increase website traffic without paid ads by getting your site ranked more highly in search engines and local search directories. Building a site that includes relevant search terms in its text – and offers extra value with helpful articles, a blog, or other useful tools – will improve your rank and encourage others to link to your site.

47. **Pay-per-Click Advertising.** You pay for these online ads each time someone clicks on one to visit your site. Costs can add up quickly, so evaluate your potential return carefully before choosing this option.

48. **Online Directories.** Listing your business in directories used by your prospective clients can increase your visibility. Some directories charge a fee to list you; others are free.

49. **Print Directories.** Use of general print directories like the Yellow Pages is waning, but consumers still turn to them in emergencies and for household services. Specialized directories for your industry or profession can be a better bet.

50. **Online Classifieds.** Best used when your business serves consumers who may be regular users of classified services such as Craigslist. Ads can be free or paid. Your ad should be narrowly targeted and ask for an immediate response, perhaps with a special offer.

51. **Newspaper or Magazine Classifieds.** May appear in the print edition, web edition, or both. Track every response you get to see whether your ads are worth the investment.

Marketing Tactics Guide: Advertising (*continued*)

52. **Banner Ads.** For these display ads on websites, in ezines, and via smartphone apps, you'll typically pay a flat fee for a length of time or per issue. Be sure you know the number of viewers who will see your ad before you buy.

53. **Print Display Ads.** Ads like these in newspapers, magazines, and trade journals are typically more for visibility than direct response. You usually need a big budget, and repeat advertising, to make them work.

54. **Event or Conference Programs.** Another visibility booster that may need a big budget. Works best if people who already know your business will notice the ad.

55. **Unsolicited Bulk Email or Text Ads.** Sending unsolicited bulk email or text message ads, otherwise known as spam, to market your professional services is probably the least effective advertising tactic you could choose, and the most likely to annoy your prospects. Just don't do it.

56. **Direct Mail.** Postal mass mailings to people who don't yet know you have nowhere near the impact of personal letters and are often a waste of money. Consider narrowing your target group and using direct contact and follow-up tactics instead.

57. **Brochure or Flyer Distribution.** Brochures and flyers can be used to develop interest with a targeted group. They can be left at a place of business your target audience frequents or posted on a bulletin board in your community.

58. **Radio or TV Ads.** You need a substantial budget to go this route. Ads must be repeated to have any effect. If you do this, get professional help in scripting and producing your ad.

59. **Billboards.** For professional services? Well, people have done it. You can probably find better ways to spend the money—like one of the other tactics already mentioned.

DEFINING YOUR BUSINESS MIX

You've got to be careful if you don't know where you're going,
because you might not get there.
– YOGI BERRA

Before you can choose the right marketing strategies and tactics to use, you need to have a clear picture of the kind of business you are wanting to build. Most service professionals offer more than one type of service, and some offer a mix of both products and services. Each line of business you offer may have a different price or different target market, so these separate business lines may require different approaches to marketing.

To begin creating a model of the business you want to have, review the three examples below.

The first "Business Mix Worksheet" shows the proposed business mix for a life coach. The coach wishes to earn a total of $100,000 per year. She's planning to have four lines of business: coaching with individual clients, paid teleseminars offered to her own audience, ebooks she sells on her website, and paid teaching and speaking that she provides to other organizations. The model below is her vision of how much she can earn from each business line to reach her desired total.

Business Mix Worksheet Example #1: Life Coach

Line of business	Desired percent of revenue	Total annual revenue desired	Amount of revenue for business line
1. Individual Coaching	72% x	100,000 =	72,000
2. Teleseminars	12% x	100,000 =	12,000
3. Ebooks	4% x	100,000 =	4,000
4. Teaching/Speaking	12% x	100,000 =	12,000
Total	100%		100,000

In the second example, a graphic designer plans to earn $75,000 per year from three different business lines: brochures and business cards, logo and identity packages, and custom illustrations. He bases his model on what percentage of his total revenue he would like each line of business to represent.

Business Mix Worksheet Example #2: Graphic Designer

Line of business	Desired percent of revenue	Total annual revenue desired	Amount of revenue for business line
1. Brochures/Biz Cards	50% x	75,000 =	37,500
2. Identity Packages	25% x	75,000 =	18,750
3. Custom Illustrations	25% x	75,000 =	18,750
Total	100%		75,000

A third example, from a personal trainer, shows a plan to earn $60,000 per year by offering a combination of individual training sessions, fitness assessment and planning, and a line of nutritional products.

Business Mix Worksheet Example #3: Personal Trainer

Line of Business	Desired percent of revenue	Total annual revenue desired	Amount of revenue for business line
1. Training Sessions	70% x	60,000 =	42,000
2. Fitness Plans	20% x	60,000 =	12,000
3. Nutritional Products	10% x	60,000 =	6,000
Total	100%		60,000

To create these business mix models, these entrepreneurs have made educated guesses about what's possible, and combined those guesses with what they want to earn. They have chosen a financial target – $75,000 or $100,000 or $60,000 per year – and estimated what it might take to get there, given the lines of business they'd like to offer.

If you've been in business for a while, you may have real numbers you can refer to in order to make estimates like these. You may already know what percentage of your business a certain line tends to be, or you may know how much you've earned from that line in the past.

If you're new, or if you're planning to make changes in how your business works or add new lines to it, you'll have less to go on. In that case, try to be realistic about your estimates.

To create an estimate of $72,000 in desired revenue per year for individual coaching, our life coach could multiply 15 ongoing clients times $400 per month times 12 months.

Our graphic designer could test his assumption that $18,750 in annual revenue is reasonable to expect for identity packages by multiplying a projected 15 identity clients per year by an average price of $1,250 (splitting the difference between $1000 packages and those priced at $1,500).

The personal trainer could assume that 20 training sessions per week for 48 weeks per year is possible, and that charging an average of $62.50 per session is reasonable (with some clients paying $75 to purchase by the session and others paying $50 for a package of sessions purchased in advance).

Use the worksheet on the next page to make your own estimates of how much revenue you'd like to have and how you think you might get there. Then test your assumptions by calculating how many clients, projects, sessions, etc., it would take to reach your goals. (An Excel version of this worksheet is available in the "Free Resources" section of www.getclientsnow.com.)

Note that you are creating a plan for only the next six months at this time, but you should use annual revenue figures to make your estimates.

Your Business Mix Worksheet

Line of Business	Desired percent of revenue		Total annual revenue desired		Amount of revenue for business line
1. _____	_____	x	_____	=	_____
2. _____	_____	x	_____	=	_____
3. _____	_____	x	_____	=	_____
4. _____	_____	x	_____	=	_____
5. _____	_____	x	_____	=	_____
Total	100%				

Line of business = List each kind of business you would like to offer over the next six months. You may choose to define your lines of business by the type of product or service you are selling, or by the distinct target markets you are selling to. If all your business is of one kind (e.g., consulting) but there are significant differences in the types of projects you would like to pursue, list each type of project separately.

Desired percent of revenue = The percentage of your total gross revenue that you would like this line of business to contribute. Must add up to 100%.

Total annual revenue desired = The total amount you would like your business to earn over the next year, for all your lines of business combined. This is your gross revenue before deducting any expenses for business overhead or the wholesale or manufacturing cost of any products you are selling.

Amount of revenue for business line = Desired percent of revenue *multiplied by* Total annual revenue desired. The amount of annual revenue you wish to bring in for each line of business.

An Excel version of this worksheet is available in the "Free Resources" section of www.getclientsnow.com.

Once you have a working model of which lines of business you'd like to offer in the next six months, decide which of those income streams you wish to create a marketing plan for right now. If some of your business already comes to you effortlessly, you might decide not to actively market for it. The graphic designer above, for example, might choose not to create a marketing plan for custom illustrations, because he finds that his brochure and identity clients often request them.

Or, you may have a sideline business that doesn't make sense to include in this marketing plan. Remember that the One-Person Marketing Plan is designed to help you sell professional services. If you are also selling a product to anyone other than your existing clients, you may wish to create an entirely separate plan for that purpose, using a different set of tools. The personal trainer above, for example, would not use the tools in this book to create a marketing plan for selling nutritional supplements to the general public. The trainer could, however, use the One-Person Marketing Plan to market these products to the clients already booking training sessions.

From this point on, remember your chosen business mix as you complete each of the exercises in this book. You are only going to be developing a marketing plan for:

- The lines of business you wish to build in the next six months
- The lines of business where you must actively work to increase or maintain your desired level of sales
- Your own professional services, or products sold to clients who already do business with you

CHOOSING WHERE TO FOCUS

Don't spend time beating on a wall, hoping to transform it into a door.
– COCO CHANEL

The next step in building your marketing plan is determining where to focus your marketing efforts. Marketing and sales for the professional services business operates on a predictable cycle, with four separate stages:

1. Filling the pipeline
2. Following up
3. Having sales conversations
4. Closing sales

The activities that take place within each stage of the cycle will vary depending on your business, but the cycle is the same for everyone. Knowing more about how this cycle works will enable you to identify exactly where to focus more time and energy in your marketing.

The diagram on page 23 illustrates this Universal Marketing Cycle as if it were a water system. At the top are collection buckets for the prospects, contacts, leads, and referrals with which you fill your marketing pipeline. On your desk, computer, or favorite handheld device, these will be represented by the names and contact information of people and organizations.

- **Prospects** are people you have reason to believe will be interested in your services.
- **Contacts** are people you meet through outreach strategies like networking, or just in the course of business and life.
- **Leads** are people you identify through research or hear about from your contacts.
- **Referrals** are people who are referred to you by contacts, clients, and others.

Your marketing pipeline empties into the follow-up pool, which you dip into in order to move potential clients and referral sources further along in the system.

The arrows in the bottom half of the diagram indicate the direction of flow. With potential clients, you want to move as quickly as possible to having a sales conversation. This is where you find out about their needs, tell them more about what you do, and see if there is a match between the two of you. When the sales conversation concludes, you may be ready to ask for the business, or you may need to prepare a detailed proposal first. The sales conversation may happen formally or informally, in person, by phone, by live chat, or even by e-mail. In some cases, the conversation stage may last 15 minutes; in others, it can take many months.

Your desired result is always the same: to move prospects forward to closing the sale. If they say yes at the end of the sales conversation, you have a new client. If they say no, they stay in the closing sales stage, where you continue to follow up with them as long as it seems worthwhile. Sometimes continued follow-up will lead directly to closing the sale after all, and at other times, you may need to have yet another sales conversation.

When the sale is closed and you begin to serve the client, you must also return the client to the follow-up pool. By continuing to follow up with this client, you may close another sale or get referrals.

Some of the people and organizations in your pipeline will never become clients, but are still potential referral sources. You should continue to follow up with those people as well.

In any of these cases, what follow-up looks like, and how often it happens, depends on the nature of your business and the type of contact that seems natural for you. Every tactic listed under Direct Contact & Follow-Up in the "59 Tactics for Marketing Your Services" list on page 6 is a potential follow-up technique.

The Universal Marketing Cycle

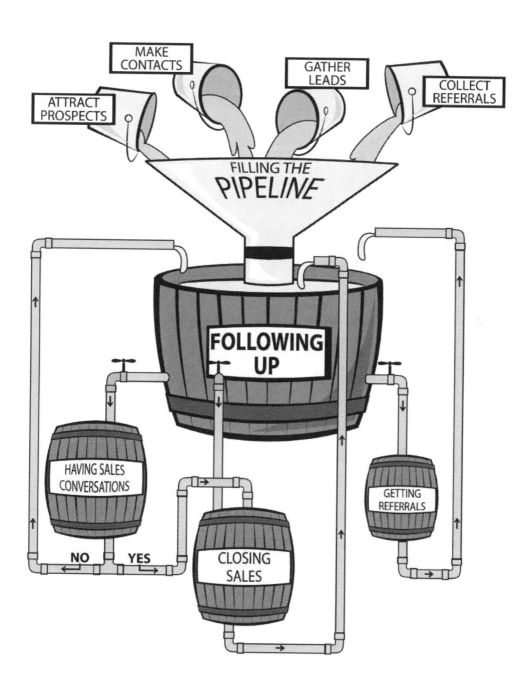

Where to Focus Your Marketing

The key to building a successful One-Person Marketing Plan is narrowing your focus to work with just one stage of the Universal Marketing Cycle at a time, even when you are pursuing many possibilities.

A brief word clarifying the terminology we are using might be helpful here. Up to this point, you have encountered marketing strategies, tactics, and types of impact. Each overall **strategy** (e.g., Direct Contact & Follow-Up) is made up of **tactics** (e.g., cold calling, warm calling, or lunch/coffee), and has a resulting **impact** (Outreach, Visibility, or Credibility). Now, you are learning about stages of the marketing cycle.

The four stages shown on the Universal Marketing Cycle diagram are:
- Filling the Pipeline (knowing enough people to contact)
- Following Up (contacting the people you already know, or know about)
- Having Sales Conversations (getting from follow-up to conversation)
- Closing Sales (getting from conversation to sale)

Think about your own situation as you review the cycle. Where in the system are you stuck? Or, what stage of your marketing needs the most work?

In most businesses, contacting prospective clients directly is one of the primary methods of follow-up, so knowing enough people to contact is an easy test to see if your pipeline is sufficiently full. But if you are in a field where direct solicitation of clients is inappropriate, such as psychotherapy or, in some cases, law, ask yourself if enough people are contacting *you*. Another good test is to imagine you were using a newsletter or e-zine for follow-up. How many people who already know you could you send it to?

If you think you may need work in more than one stage of the cycle, start with the first one in the sequence. For example, if you feel stuck on both Following Up and Having Sales Conversations, choose Following Up. If you aren't at all sure where to start, begin with Filling the Pipeline. If that's not really where the problem is, you will find out soon enough and move forward to the right stage anyway. Just be sure to pick only one.

What Strategies Should You Use?

On the next page, check the "Where Are You Stuck?" box that corresponds to the marketing stage you have chosen. This is the area you will focus on as you design and implement your marketing plan.

Now look at the "What Should You Do?" section that matches the box you checked. This will tell you what marketing strategies you should focus on using. The strategies recommended for each stage are listed from most to least effective. Direct Contact and Follow-Up plus Networking and Referral Building are considered to be the most effective approaches overall, regardless of which stage you are in. While any of the strategies listed for your stage will work, the ones listed first in each case are most likely to produce results with the least struggle. It's a good idea to employ the most effective strategies, unless there is some reason that a particular strategy won't work well for you. If you are nervous about speaking in public, for example, you might choose Writing and Publicity as an alternative to add more credibility to your approach.

Choose at least two, but no more than four, strategies for your marketing plan now. You may wish to look at the list of "59 Tactics for Marketing Your Services" in the "What Is Marketing?" chapter to help you choose which strategies your plan should focus on.

If you're having trouble deciding, consider questions like: Which of them do you most want to do? Which seem the most interesting? Which have you seen other professionals in your field use successfully? Which do you have the resources in time and money to tackle right now?

Then write your chosen strategies at the bottom of the next page.

Where Are You Stuck?

- ☐ Filling the pipeline
- ☐ Following up
- ☐ Having sales conversations
- ☐ Closing the sale

What Should You Do?

If you chose Filling the Pipeline...

You should use the strategies: *For the impact:*
1. Direct Contact and Follow-Up   Outreach
2. Networking and Referral Building   Outreach and Credibility

Plus no more than one or two of the following:
3. Public Speaking   Visibility and Credibility
4. Writing and Publicity   Visibility and Credibility
5. Promotional Events   Visibility
6. Advertising   Visibility

CHOOSING WHERE TO FOCUS

If you chose Following Up...

You should use the strategies:	*For the impact:*
1. Direct contact and follow-up	Outreach
2. Networking and referral building	Outreach and Credibility

If you chose Having Sales Conversations...

You should use the strategies:	*For the impact:*
1. Direct contact and follow-up	Outreach
2. Networking and referral building	Outreach and Credibility

Plus no more than one of the following:	
3. Public speaking	Visibility and Credibility
4. Writing and publicity	Visibility and Credibility
5. Promotional events	Visibility

If you chose Closing Sales...

You should use the strategies:	*For the impact:*
1. Direct contact and follow-up	Outreach
2. Networking and referral building	Outreach and Credibility

Plus no more than one of the following:	
3. Public speaking	Visibility and Credibility
4. Writing and publicity	Visibility and Credibility

Which Strategies Will You Use?

1. _____

2. _____

3. _____

4. _____

WEIGHTING YOUR STRATEGIES

I find that the harder I work, the more luck I seem to have.
— Thomas Jefferson

Now that you know which marketing strategies will be included in your plan, look at the two circles on the next page. Each circle represents a pie that is divided in slices. Each slice represents the relative weight, or level of effort, to be devoted to the activities named in the pie.

The first pie represents the impact to be created with your marketing plan. The example shows an impact evenly divided into Outreach and Credibility.

To determine which types of impact are appropriate for you, refer to the "What Should You Do?" chart on the previous two pages. Then divide up your own "Impact" pie on page 29 into slices that represent the level of effort you are going to devote to each impact. If the pie is equal to 100% of your marketing effort, what percentage does each impact deserve?

If you are working on Filling the Pipeline, for example, you could choose 33% Outreach, 33% Credibility, and 33% Visibility, or, because Outreach is more effective than either of the others, 50% Outreach, 25% Credibility, and 25% Visibility. If you are stuck in the "Following Up" stage, you could choose 50% Outreach and 50% Credibility, as in the example.

Use your own judgment. Is there one area you have previously neglected more than the other? You could put your effort there. Is there one area where you feel more motivated to take action? That is also a good way to choose.

If you are stuck in Having Sales Conversations or Closing Sales, you could slice up your pie into thirds, or let the relative effectiveness of each impact guide you to creating a 50/35/15 pie, or 60/30/10.

The important thing to know here is that it doesn't matter so much *what* you choose as it does *that* you choose. Pick what feels right to you. You can always adjust it later on.

Marketing Strategy Pie Example

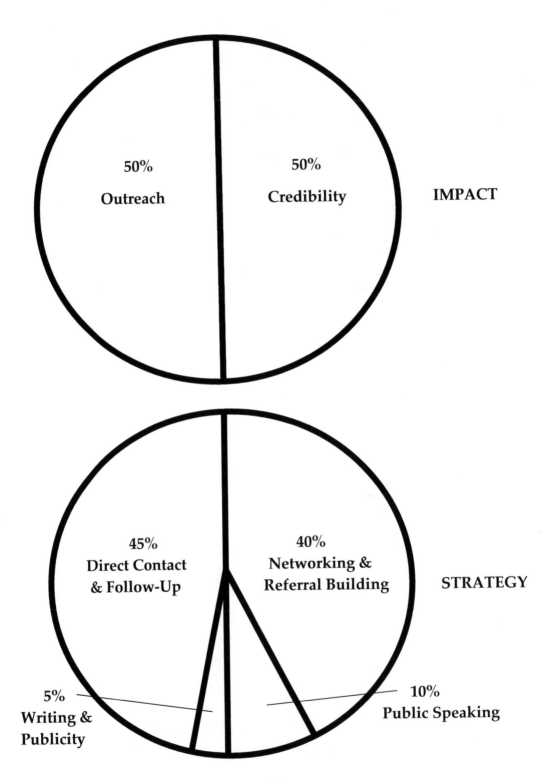

50%
Outreach

50%
Credibility

IMPACT

45%
Direct Contact
& Follow-Up

40%
Networking &
Referral Building

STRATEGY

5%
Writing &
Publicity

10%
Public Speaking

Your Marketing Strategy Pie

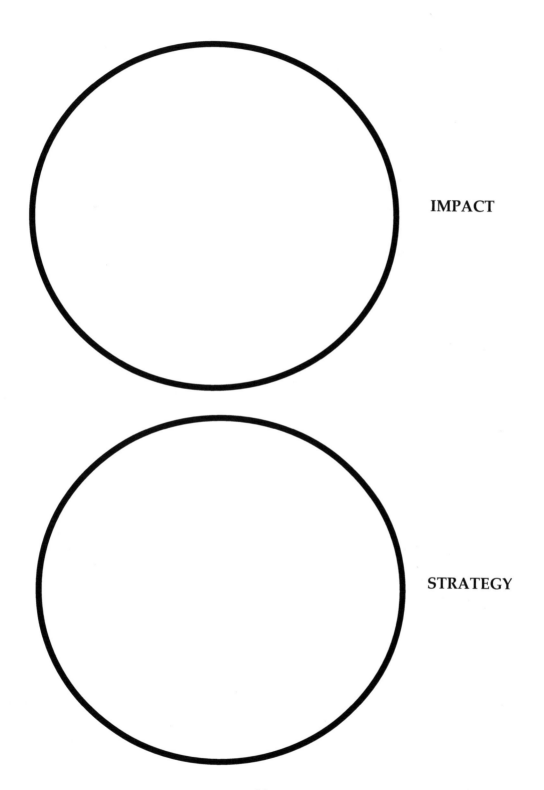

IMPACT

STRATEGY

Slicing the Strategy Pie

Once your "Impact" pie is divided into slices, you're ready to slice up your "Strategy" pie. Use the "What Should You Do?" chart in the previous chapter to remind you which impact each strategy creates. Then take the two to four marketing strategies you chose at the end of that chapter and assign a relative level of effort to each one that will allow you to create the impact you desire. The sample "Strategy" pie on page 28 shows an assigned level of effort for four different strategies.

Again, it doesn't matter so much *what* you choose as *that* you choose. You already know you are working on the right area of marketing, because you went through all the steps above. Just remember to divide up your "Strategy" pie to match your "Impact" pie.

If your "Impact" pie shows 100% Outreach, you should be using only Direct Contact & Follow-Up and Networking & Referral Building as strategies. If your "Impact" pie shows 50% Visibility, the Visibility-only strategies you choose should add up to no more than 50%. When a strategy has more than one impact (for example, Public Speaking has the impact of both Credibility and Visibility), you can include it in either category, or divide it between them.

Also, you are choosing only strategies right now, not tactics, so you will have more opportunities for fine-tuning your plan later on.

SELECTING A TARGET MARKET

Go to your bosom: knock there, and ask your heart what it doth know.
– WILLIAM SHAKESPEARE

So far in this book, you have defined your **business mix**, determined what **stage** of the Universal Marketing Cycle to focus on, chosen which marketing **strategies** to use, and given each strategy a relative weight. In a few pages, you will be making choices about the **tactics** and **tools** you will use in your marketing plan.

To help you make the best possible choices, it will be useful to take a look at your **target market**. This is the group of people or organizations you will actively pursue with your marketing plan.

The function of having a target market is not to limit who you can do business with; it's to help you organize and concentrate your efforts. Without a defined target market, your marketing will be diluted and haphazard. You can still do business with anyone who shows an interest in what you offer. Your target market, though, is who you will actively pursue and build your plan around.

If you're not sure who your target market is, try asking yourself the questions listed under one or both of the approaches suggested below.

Choose the market you like most	Find the market most in need
Whose problems and goals do you truly care about?	What market needs your service the most or has hired you most often?
Who do you enjoy spending time with?	Who has given you repeat business and/or referred others?
Who has been the most satisfying type of client in the past?	Who is easily able to pay what you plan to charge?
Who has paid their bills promptly?	Who is most likely to give you large contracts or ongoing business?
Who has been easiest to work with?	What market is currently growing in size or earning power?
Who do you most want to serve, or where can you best make an impact?	In what market will future trends likely cause an increased need?
Where do you already have many contacts or an established reputation?	What market might be the easiest for you to sell to?

Qualifying and Labeling Your Market

When you've identified one or more groups that seem to fit, use these questions to see if they qualify as a good target market for you:

- Are there enough people or organizations within your desired geographic area for this market to support your business?
- Do they have a pre-existing, identifiable need for what you offer?
- Can they pay you what you need to charge?
- Can you afford to reach them with the marketing methods you have available?

Once you have selected a target market, the "Client Profile" worksheets on the following two pages will help you describe your market in a concrete way. It's important to give your target market a label that describes them as precisely as possible. Defining a group by identifiable characteristics will help you know where to look for them, or tell others who would be a good client to refer to you.

A contract trainer specializing in conflict resolution skills, for example, would find little value in defining her target market as "organizations that experience conflict." This won't help her focus her marketing, as it could be anyone.

"Organizations in need of conflict resolution training" won't do the job as a definition either. Could you look them up in a directory? Would a referral source know who would be a good lead for you? Could you figure out where these people would go to network? No. You can't do any of these things with a need-based definition.

But if the trainer defined her market as "human resource development or training managers in midsize to large companies located in the Boston area," now she can find them – and so can anyone she knows who might refer business to her.

When you have more than one target market, be careful to define each one separately rather than lumping them together. For example, it's more effective to target "financial planners and money managers" than to identify your target generically as "professional partnerships" or "financial services firms."

If your target market is individuals, fill out the "Individual Client Profile" on the next page. If you plan to target organizations, fill out the "Organizational Client Profile" on the second page following.

Most of the information on the profile worksheets is demographic. These are the defining characteristics of your target population. If there is an important characteristic which the demographics don't address, you can also include information about psychographics or conditions. For individuals, you might list "career transition" as one of their "Interests." For organizations, you might list "currently downsizing" under "Special Characteristics."

Individual Client Profile

AGE
☐ Teens ☐ College students ☐ 20-35 ☐ 36-50 ☐ 51-65
☐ Retirees ☐ Seniors

GENDER
☐ Female ☐ Male

FAMILY STATUS
☐ Single ☐ Married ☐ Domestic partners
☐ Childless ☐ Young children ☐ Parents ☐ Grandparents

OCCUPATION
☐ Student ☐ Support staff ☐ Blue collar ☐ Professionals
☐ Technical ☐ Sales ☐ Managers ☐ Executives
☐ Self-employed ☐ CEOs ☐ Unemployed ☐ Retired

INCOME
☐ Individual ☐ Household ☐ < 10,000 ☐ $10-25,000
☐ $26-50,000 ☐ $51-100,000 ☐ $101-250,000 ☐ $251-500,000
☐ $501-1,000,000 ☐ > $1,000,000

GEOGRAPHIC LOCATION
☐ Neighborhood: ☐ City/County:
☐ State/Province/Region: ☐ Country:

EDUCATION
☐ High School ☐ Some College ☐ College Grad ☐ Post Graduate

INTERESTS/HOBBIES/AFFINITY GROUPS

Organizational Client Profile

CLASSIFICATION
□ Retailer   □ Manufacturer   □ Wholesaler/Distributor
□ Service Provider   □ Government   □ Nonprofit
□ Educational Institution   □ Other:

INDUSTRY

NUMBER OF EMPLOYEES
□ 1-10   □ 11-50   □ 51-100   □ 101-500
□ 501-1,000   □ 1,001-5,000   □ 5,001-10,000   □ 10,001-50,000
□ 50,001-100,000   □ > 100,000

ANNUAL REVENUE
□ < $50K   □ $51-100K   □ $101-250K   □ $251-500K
□ $501K-1 million   □ $1.1-5 million   □ $5.1-10 million
□ $11-50 million   □ $51-100 million   □ > $100 million

LEGAL FORM
□ Proprietorship   □ Partnership/LLC   □ Private Corporation
□ Public Corporation   □ Association   □ Family-Owned
□ Other:

GEOGRAPHIC LOCATION
□ Neighborhood: □ City/County:
□ State/Province/Region: □ Country:
□ Multiple Domestic Locations   □ Multiple International Locations

SPECIAL CHARACTERISTICS

DECISION MAKERS
Division/Department:
Position Title:
Rank in Company:

SETTING MARKETING GOALS

Aim at a high mark and you'll hit it. No, not the first time, nor the second time.
Maybe not the third. But keep on aiming and keep on shooting
for only practice will make you perfect.
– ANNIE OAKLEY

To build an effective marketing plan, you must have a realistic picture of the effort required to reach your financial goals. To bring in the amount of revenue you want, you will need to close a certain number of sales each month. To land one sale, you must typically have sales conversations with several different potential clients. To find just one person to have a conversation with, you must typically make contact with several different prospects.

Knowing the number of prospects and sales conversations you are likely to need on a monthly basis will help you quantify your marketing plan. This is important, because without a clear idea of how much marketing you actually need, you may be doing all the right things to market your business, but not doing enough of them. Service providers frequently underestimate the number of prospects they should have in the pipeline at any one time. As you will see in the calculations below, it is not uncommon to need as many as 30 prospects for each sale that you ultimately make.

Use the worksheet below to calculate the number of sales, sales conversations, and prospects you will need each month to earn the amount of revenue you desire. (An Excel version of this worksheet is available in the "Free Resources" section of www.getclientsnow.com.)

To determine the various elements required by this worksheet, remember that you are building your marketing plan for only:

- The lines of business where you must actively work to increase or maintain your desired level of sales
- Your own professional services, or products sold to clients who already do business with you

Important Note: If you decide to build a marketing plan that includes more than one line of business, complete a Marketing Goals Worksheet for each line of business *separately*. You will add up the total number of sales conversations and prospects on all your Marketing Goals Worksheets when you complete the Marketing Plan Worksheet later on.

Marketing Goals Worksheet Example #1: Life Coach

Line of Business: Individual Coaching

Desired monthly revenue	$6,000
divided by Amount of average sale	$2,400*
= Number of sales needed per month	2.5
times Number of sales conversations needed per sale	3
= Number of sales conversations needed per month	7.5
times Number of prospects needed per sales conversation	10
= Number of prospects needed per month	75

* Average sale derived from $400 per client per month over 6 months

Marketing Goals Worksheet Example #2: Graphic Designer

Line of Business: Identity Packages

Desired monthly revenue	$1,562
divided by Amount of average sale	$1,250*
= Number of sales needed per month	1.25
times Number of sales conversations needed per sale	3
= Number of sales conversations needed per month	3.75
times Number of prospects needed per sales conversation	10
= Number of prospects needed per month	38

* Average sale derived from package prices ranging from $1,000-1,500

Marketing Goals Worksheet Example #3: Personal Trainer

Line of Business: Training Sessions

Desired monthly revenue	$3,500
divided by Amount of average sale	$1,625*
= Number of sales needed per month	2.2
times Number of sales conversations needed per sale	3
= Number of sales conversations needed per month	6.6
times Number of prospects needed per sales conversation	10
= Number of prospects needed per month	66

* Average sale derived from $50-75 per weekly session over 26 weeks

Your Marketing Goals Worksheet

Line of Business: _____

Desired monthly revenue   _____
divided by Amount of average sale   _____

= Number of sales needed per month   _____
times Number of sales conversations needed per sale   _____

= Number of sales conversations needed per month _____

times Number of prospects needed per sales conversation _____

= Number of prospects needed per month   _____

An Excel version of this worksheet is available in the "Free Resources" section of www.getclientsnow.com.

Desired monthly revenue = The amount of gross revenue you want to earn from this line of business each month. If your revenue fluctuates, divide your annual revenue by 12 to get a monthly average. If you work on commission, use the dollar amount of sales you need each month to earn the level of commissions you want.

Amount of average sale = How much money in total the average client spends each time they decide to buy (even if this amount is paid over many months). If your business is new, look at your pricing and make your best guess of what your average sale will be. If your business is established, look at last year's sales records to make an estimate. If you can't calculate an accurate average sale amount, but you already know how many new clients you need each month to reach your revenue goal, just skip to the next step, and use that number as *number of sales*.

Number of sales needed = *Desired monthly revenue* divided by *amount of average sale*. This is the number of sales you must make each month to reach your revenue goal. If a typical sale results in revenue over many months, it is possible to have a fractional number here. In other words, you may need to make a new sale less than once a month. On the other hand, if you have a low average sale amount, you may have a high number of monthly sales required.

Your Marketing Goals Worksheet (*continued*)

Number of sales conversations needed per sale = This is the number of prospects you must have sales conversations with in order to get one sale. A sales conversation is defined as an interactive exchange where you give full details about your service, and ask for the business. Don't confuse sales conversations with follow-up interactions, which might happen before or after a sales conversation. You are counting people with this number, not conversations. So if you have a sales conversation with the same prospect more than once, it still counts as only one conversation. If you don't know what this number is for you, assume 3 until you learn otherwise.

Number of sales conversations needed = *Number of sales needed* multiplied by *number of sales conversations needed per sale*. This is the number of sales conversations you must have each month to reach your sales goal. You will use this number to build your marketing plan.

Number of prospects per sales conversation = This is the number of people you must make contact with to land one sales conversation. If you don't know what this number is, assume 10.

Number of prospects needed per month = *Number of sales conversations needed* multiplied by *number of prospects per sales conversation*. This is the number of people you must contact (or who must contact you) each month to meet your sales goal. You will use this number to build your marketing plan.

If the number of prospects and sales conversations you need each month seems high, don't panic! Stick with this planning process and you will find out whether or not your revenue goal is realistic.

It may be necessary for you to use marketing approaches that allow you to make contact with larger numbers of people than you initially thought. Remember, too, that the entire calculation is based on the amount of your average sale. Perhaps your rates need to be higher, or you need to choose a target market which will offer you larger projects or repeat business. Part of the value of building a marketing plan is that the process requires checking out many of your assumptions about how your business should work.

CHOOSING A MARKETING BUDGET

"Time is money," says the proverb, but turn it around and you get a precious truth.
Money is time.
– GEORGE GISSING

Now that you know how many prospects you must make contact with each month in order to reach your revenue goal, you'll need to determine how much time and money you have available to spend on marketing. This will allow you to see the amount of resources you can afford to spend on each prospect, which in turn will help you determine which marketing tactics to use.

If you are building a marketing plan that includes more than one line of business, complete these worksheets for your entire business, not for each line separately. (Excel versions of these worksheets are available in the "Free Resources" section of www.getclientsnow.com.)

Budgeting Marketing Time

Use the worksheet below to figure out what your marketing budget is for time – the number of hours you have available.

Marketing Hours Worksheet Example

Monthly number of hours you have available to spend on your business	176
minus Hours needed to serve existing clients	103
minus Hours needed to run the business	33
= Hours available for marketing	40
divided by Number of prospects needed	60
= Hours available per prospect	.66 (40 min.)

Your Marketing Hours Worksheet

Number of hours you have available monthly   _____
to spend on your business

minus Hours needed to serve existing clients   _____

minus Hours needed to run the business   _____

= Hours available for marketing   _____

divided by Number of prospects needed   _____

= Hours available per prospect   _____

Number of hours you have available monthly = If you have no other job, this is the number of hours you wish to work each month. If you are not yet full time in your business, this is the number of hours you can set aside each month for it.

Hours needed to serve clients = Number of hours per month you spend on client service now. You will increase this as you get more clients. If you don't know what this number is, start tracking it now, and meanwhile, make your best guess.

Hours required to run the business = Number of hours per month you must spend on managing, administering, accounting, correspondence, product development, and learning. Again, if you don't know what this number is, start tracking it. A good starting estimate is often 20% of the total hours available.

Hours available for marketing = *Number of hours you have available* minus *hours needed to serve clients* minus *hours required to run the business*. Number of hours per month you have available for all your marketing activities. You can reduce this as you get more clients (but never to zero). This number is the total number of hours you will be dividing up, using your "Marketing Strategy Pie."

Number of prospects needed = Prospect goal from your completed Marketing Goals Worksheet. This is the number of prospects your plan must generate.

Hours available per prospect = *Hours available for marketing* divided by *number of prospects needed*. Number of hours you have available to spend on each prospect. This will guide you to selecting tactics that fit the time you have available.

Budgeting Marketing Money

You will also need to budget the money you will spend on marketing. One way to set a financial budget is simply to look at how much you have available. Another way is to estimate how much would really be needed to build your business to the level you want. Using this second method may encourage you to spend more than you originally intended (if that's what it will take), or it may prevent you from overspending if a higher marketing budget doesn't seem warranted.

Use the worksheet below to calculate what an appropriate financial budget might be. Then make your own choice about how much you wish to – and can afford to – spend.

Marketing Money Worksheet Example

Projected monthly gross revenue	$6,000
times Percentage allocated to marketing	10%
= Monthly marketing budget	600
divided by Number of prospects needed	60
= Money available per prospect	$10.00

Your Marketing Money Worksheet

Projected monthly gross revenue   _____

times Percentage allocated to marketing   _____

= Monthly marketing budget   _____

divided by Number of prospects needed   _____

= Money available per prospect   _____

Projected monthly gross revenue = Amount of money you plan to bring in from your business each month when you are making the number of sales you want. This should be the annual total shown at the bottom of your completed Business Mix Worksheet, divided by 12. Do not deduct any expenses or taxes. It is important to use your revenue goal rather than your current revenue to calculate your marketing budget. In marketing, you need to spend for the level of business you want, not the level of business you have.

Percentage allocated to marketing = Amount of your gross revenue you wish to spend on marketing, expressed as a percentage. In a professional services business, this number is typically no less than 4% and no more than 12%. A good number for a new consultant, coach, or professional building a practice is 10%.

Monthly marketing budget = *Projected monthly gross revenue* multiplied by *percentage allocated to marketing*. This is the recommended amount for you to spend on marketing each month. You can choose to use this number or not, but do set a firm budget, then allow it to guide you in choosing appropriate marketing tactics for the amount you wish to spend.

Number of prospects needed = The prospect goal from your completed Marketing Goals Worksheet. This is the number of prospects per month your plan must generate.

Money available per prospect = *Monthly marketing budget* divided by *number of prospects needed*. Amount you have available to spend on each prospect. This will guide you to selecting tactics that fit your available budget.

DEFINING YOUR MARKETING TACTICS

Creative minds have always been known to survive any amount of bad training.
— ANNA FREUD

With the "Marketing Strategy Pie," you made choices about which marketing **strategies** to include in your plan, and how much of each one. In the worksheets that followed, you set goals and boundaries for **prospects, sales conversations, hours,** and **money**. Now it's time to choose the individual **tactics** you will use to implement your marketing strategies and achieve your goals.

Refer to the list of marketing tactics beginning on page 6. Look only at those sections that apply to the strategies you intend to use – the strategies you chose on page 26. Begin selecting from those sections the specific tactics you would like to include in your marketing plan.

Here are some good reasons to choose a particular tactic:
- It's easy, or you like doing it (which means you will do it)
- It fits within your time and money budget
- It would generate the number of prospects you need
- You see that it would be particularly effective with your target market
- It's something you've seen other successful professionals do

Here are some good reasons *not* to choose a particular tactic:
- It's so hard or distasteful that you will avoid it completely and sabotage your plan
- It would cost more money than you have to spend
- It would exceed your "hours available per prospect" budget
- You've never seen anyone use it with your target market, or never seen another professional in your field use it (maybe there's a reason)

On the "Marketing Tactics Worksheet" on the following page, list the tactics you think you might use under each of the strategies shown. If you are not planning to use a particular strategy at present, leave that section blank.

Don't worry if you seem to be selecting too many tactics right now. This is only the first cut, and you will be eliminating some later on.

Your Marketing Tactics Worksheet

Direct Contact & Follow-Up

Networking & Referral Building

Public Speaking

Writing & Publicity

Promotional Events

Advertising

SELECTING YOUR MARKETING TOOLS

The expectations of life depend upon diligence;
the mechanic that would perfect his work must first sharpen his tools.
– CONFUCIUS

The final element to be added to your marketing plan is a selection of the **tools** that you will need in order to employ the **tactics** you have chosen. On the next page, there is a list of 57 tools to choose from, followed by a guide to the tools.

Here are some good reasons to choose a particular tool:

- You need it to implement a tactic you wish to use
- You believe it would help you get your marketing "unstuck" in the stage of the Universal Marketing Cycle you are focusing on
- You can afford the time and money needed to create it
- You see that it would be particularly effective with your target market
- Every successful professional in your field seems to have one

Here are some good reasons *not* to choose a particular tool:

- None of the tactics you chose requires it
- It doesn't address the stage of marketing where you are most stuck
- It will take more time and/or money than you have to spend
- You've never seen another professional like you use it

Look first at the tools listed for the stage of the marketing cycle you are currently working on (e.g., Following Up). It's possible you may also need to look at the stage before your current stage if it seems there is an important tool you are still missing.

On the "Marketing Tools Worksheet" on page 54, list the tools you think you will need to implement your tactics, then estimate how much time and money it will take to create each one.

Notice that some of the choices listed are skills, rather than tangible items. When estimating how much time and money you might need in order to acquire a particular skill, assume that what you are striving for is simply an adequate skill level rather than complete mastery.

It's okay to list more tools than your monthly time and money budget allows, if you are willing to spread out your "tool-making" projects over two or more months. Just remember that if a tool is really necessary to use a particular tactic, you won't be able to use that tactic until the tool is in place.

57 Tools for Marketing Your Services

Filling the Pipeline
- Description of Services
- Market Niche Definition
- 10-Second Introduction
- Business Cards
- Self-Confidence Skills
- Website
- Social Media Profile/Page
- Prospect List
- Lead Sources
- Live Networking Venues
- Online Networking Venues
- Networking Skills
- Referral Partners
- Speaking Venues
- Speaking Topics/Bio
- Writing/Publishing Venues
- Articles or Writing Queries
- Blog Theme/Topics
- Publicity Venues
- Press Release/Media Kit
- Photos/Audio/Video
- Promotion Concept
- Promotion Plan
- Advertising Venues
- Flyer Venues
- Ad Copy, Layout, or Script

Following Up
- Contact Management System
- 30-Second Commercial
- Brochure
- Marketing Kit
- Model Marketing Letter
- In-House Mailing List
- Postcard or Mailer
- Newsletter or Ezine
- Broadcast Email System

57 Tools for Marketing Your Services: Following Up (*continued*)

- Bonus for Online Subscribers
- Personal Connections

Having Sales Conversations
- Telemarketing Script/Skills
- Qualifying Questions
- Higher Quality Leads and Referrals
- Better Website Conversion
- Professional Visibility
- Competitive Research
- Target Market Research
- New Market Position
- Better Service Package
- Narrower Focus of Services

Closing Sales
- Professional Credibility
- Testimonials or References
- Better-Qualified Prospects
- Stronger Relationships
- Presentation Script/Visuals
- Presentation Skills
- Portfolio
- Leave-Behind
- Selling Script
- Selling Skills

Marketing Tools Guide

Filling the Pipeline

1. **Description of Services.** A clear, specific description of the features, benefits, structure, and cost of the primary services you will focus on in your marketing.
2. **Market Niche Definition.** Description of the target market you most wish to do business with and the niche area in which you specialize.
3. **10-Second Introduction.** Self-introduction that describes what you do and who you do it for in a clear and memorable way.
4. **Business Cards.** To include your contact information and a brief summary of what you offer, such as a position title, specialties, tag line, or key benefit.
5. **Self-Confidence Skills.** A higher level of confidence and key self-confidence tools to help you overcome fear, resistance, and self-doubt when marketing yourself.
6. **Website.** A basic site that tells visitors what you do and why they should hire you, or a more powerful site that offers free resources and captures visitors' contact information.
7. **Social Media Profile/Page.** A profile for yourself or a page for your business that allows you to become active in social media networks or just be found more easily online.
8. **Prospect List.** List of people or companies in your target market that you purchase, compile, or acquire from a lead source.
9. **Lead Sources.** Groups, institutions, publications, websites, media sources, and networking contacts that can give you information about potential clients on a regular basis.
10. **Live Networking Venues.** Places, groups, and events where you can go in person to meet prospective clients and referral partners.
11. **Online Networking Venues.** Social media networks, message boards, discussion groups, web chats, and blogs where you can meet and follow up with people online.
12. **Networking Skills.** Techniques or experience to help you feel more comfortable about meeting people and interacting with them to build relationships.
13. **Referral Partners.** People, groups, or institutions that have contact with your target market and are willing to refer potential clients to you on a regular basis.
14. **Speaking Venues.** Places, groups, or events – live or online – where you might be able to speak to promote your business.

Marketing Tools Guide: Filling the Pipeline (*continued*)

15. **Speaking Topics/Bio.** Description of one to three topics you are available to speak on, plus a summary of your background and speaking experience.
16. **Writing/Publishing Venues.** Publications, blogs, or websites for which you can write articles, tips, guest blog posts, or an ongoing column.
17. **Articles or Writing Queries.** Articles, tips, or blog posts you want to have published, or queries about pieces you'd like to write.
18. **Blog Theme/Topics.** A concept for your blog that will give it a sustainable theme, and a series of topics you might blog about.
19. **Publicity Venues.** Print, broadcast, email, and web media outlets you can approach to get quoted, interviewed, or profiled.
20. **Press Release/Media Kit.** A release is the bulletin you send media outlets to attract press coverage. A media kit – print or online – provides more in-depth details about you.
21. **Photos/Audio/Video.** Visual or audio samples to supplement your publicity efforts and demonstrate your expertise.
22. **Promotion Concept.** Idea for a promotional event, such as a free demonstration or workshop, complimentary teleclass or webinar, or an exhibit at a trade show.
23. **Promotion Plan.** Your plan for producing a promotional event or trade show appearance.
24. **Advertising Venues.** Places you can advertise to reach your prospects: e.g., direct mail, print publications, directories, websites, search engines, ezines, or broadcast email.
25. **Flyer Venues.** Places where you can post, distribute, or circulate a flyer.
26. **Ad Copy, Layout, or Script.** What your proposed ad will say and how it will look.

Following Up

27. **Contact Management System.** Organized method to keep track of all your contacts. Could be a notebook, desktop software, a cloud application, or a smartphone/tablet app.
28. **30-Second Commercial.** Brief verbal summary of what you do, who you do it for, and key benefits and results you deliver.
29. **Brochure.** Printed summary of the services you offer, benefits of working with you, and your qualifications.
30. **Marketing Kit.** Expanded brochure with multiple pieces (e.g., professional bio, client list, testimonial letters, or articles).

Marketing Tools Guide: Following Up (*continued*)

31. **Model Marketing Letter.** Boilerplate language you modify to create letters you send to contacts, rather than writing each one from scratch.
32. **In-House Mailing List.** List of clients, prospects, and referral partners whose names you have accumulated from networking, referrals, visits to your website, speaking, etc.
33. **Postcard or Mailer.** Marketing literature you send by postal mail to remind prospects that you are still around, or make a special offer.
34. **Newsletter or Ezine.** Collection of articles, tips, and/or announcements you periodically send by postal mail or email.
35. **Broadcast Email System.** System that allows website visitors to subscribe to your email list, and allows you to send them email broadcasts or autoresponses.
36. **Bonus for Online Subscribers.** Free gift you provide website visitors as an incentive to subscribe to your email list, e.g., an ebook, white paper, or video tutorial.
37. **Personal Connections.** Connections between you and prospects that encourage them to speak with you, e.g., referrals, introductions, or memberships you share.

Having Sales Conversations

38. **Telemarketing Script/Skills.** Better language and techniques to help you improve at selling yourself by phone.
39. **Qualifying Questions.** Questions to ask your prospects to determine whether they are likely candidates for your services.
40. **Higher Quality Leads and Referrals.** The types of prospects who are most likely to buy, based on their profile or the source of the original lead.
41. **Better Website Conversion.** Revisions to your website that encourage visitors to stay longer, return again, or contact you to discuss your services.
42. **Professional Visibility.** Making yourself more visible in your market niche to increase the likelihood that prospects know your name before you contact them.
43. **Competitive Research.** Information about the competition that enables you to better compete by emulating what works and improving on what doesn't.
44. **Target Market Research.** Information about your prospective clients that tells you more about what they want and need.
45. **New Market Position.** Influencing how prospects think of you in comparison to your competition by changing your marketing messages.

Marketing Tools Guide: Having Sales Conversations (*continued*)

46. **Better Service Package.** A different way of packaging your services or fees to make them more attractive to prospective clients.
47. **Narrower Focus of Services.** Limiting what you offer your prospects to the one or two lines of business that your prospects are most likely to buy.

Closing Sales

48. **Professional Credibility.** How prospects perceive your ability to perform, based on what they see of your background, experience, credentials, or expertise.
49. **Testimonials or References.** Letters or quotes from satisfied clients, or a list of verifiable references with their contact information.
50. **Better-Qualified Prospects.** Prospects who are predisposed to become clients because of their needs, desires, or ability to pay.
51. **Stronger Relationships.** Building connection and trust over time through exposure to you, your abilities, or others who already trust you.
52. **Presentation Script/Visuals.** An outline of what you plan to discuss in sales conversations and supporting visuals to make your services more tangible.
53. **Presentation Skills.** Techniques or experience you need to get more comfortable with questioning, listening, or presenting.
54. **Portfolio.** Tangible examples of your work that you can show to a prospect, e.g., case studies, photographs, videos, or samples of designs, writing, or reports.
55. **Leave-Behind.** Something extra you leave with, or send to, a prospect to use or review after a sales conversation.
56. **Selling Script.** A list of talking points to remember when closing the sale, including asking-for-the-business questions, and answers to common objections.
57. **Selling Skills.** Techniques or experience to help you do a better job at closing the sale.

Your Marketing Tools Worksheet

<u>Marketing Tool</u>   **<u>Time Needed</u>**   **<u>Money Needed</u>**

CREATING YOUR MARKETING PLAN

You've got to think about big things while you're doing small things,
so that all the small things go in the right direction.
– ALVIN TOFFLER

At this point in the planning process, you know which **strategies** you plan to use, how many **prospects** and **sales conversations** you need, the number of **hours** and **money** you have available to spend, the **tactics** you would like to employ, and the **tools** you need to create. It's time to put it all together into a six-month marketing plan. We'll begin by making a plan for a **model month**. (See page 61 for an example.)

A model month is what your marketing plan will look like when all of your tactics are fully employed. If you are just beginning to actively market, some tactics won't be effective right away because they need preparation and lead time in order to pay off. For example, in order to make warm calls to prospects, you must have already met the prospects, perhaps by networking or speaking. In order to send out reminder postcards, you must have already made some initial contacts by phone or in person.

Once you have built a marketing plan for your model month, you will then be able to work backward and see exactly what needs to be done in Months 1, 2, 3, and so on.

Planning Your Model Month

Print a copy of the full-sized blank worksheet on page 64 or download the Excel version from the "Free Resources" section of www.getclientsnow.com. Fill in the information you know already: **revenue** and **sales goals**, number of **prospects** and **sales conversations** needed, **hours** available, **money** available, and the marketing **strategies** you plan to use. There are descriptions of each item on pages 59-60, and a completed example on page 61.

In order to determine which **tactics** to include in your plan, you will need to do some modeling. Pick a tactic on your completed Marketing Tactics Worksheet, e.g., "warm calling," and try to quantify it. How many warm calls should you make each month? How much time will that take? What will it cost? How many actual contacts with prospective clients will it generate? How many sales conversations? It's perfectly okay to guess at these answers – everybody does at first. You will be testing them out later on.

Once you've quantified a tactic, divide the total amount of time and money it will require by the number of prospects you believe it will generate. If the result is equal to or less than your "Hours Available per Prospect" or "Money Available per Prospect," it passes the first test and can stay on your list. If it doesn't, scratch it and go on to the next potential tactic on your worksheet. Here's an example of a quantified tactic that would pass this test:

Marketing tactic	How often How many	Hours	Money	Prospects	Sales convs
Warm calls to contacts	8/week = 32	6.5	0	10	3

6.5 hours *divided by* **10 prospects = .65 hours per prospect**
Hours available per prospect (from the Marketing Hours Worksheet) = .66

When you have screened each of your possible tactics with this initial test, add up the hours and money that would be required, and the number of prospects and presentations that would result, if you used all your chosen tactics. If you have enough hours and money available to do them all, the number of prospects and presentations is enough to meet your target, and the percentage of time you will spend on each tactic more or less matches up with the strategies you initially chose, you have the right list.

If not, you must prioritize. Which tactics are most likely to generate the number of prospects you need while staying within your time and money budget? Keep modeling until you have a mix of tactics that works.

In selecting **tools**, your task is a bit easier. You can create all the tools listed on your completed Marketing Tools Worksheet, you just can't create them all at once. Give first priority to the ones you will need on an ongoing basis to implement the tactics you are using. If you are going to do a monthly postcard mailing, for example, creating the postcards is a must! Then include some time to be set aside each month for one-time projects, such as setting up your contact management system or developing a 10-second introduction.

Do the tool-making projects you listed fit within your total time and money budget? If so, they stay on. If not, reprioritize, just as you did with the tactics. You can "borrow" money from upcoming months if you need to spend extra money on tools at the beginning, but since you can't borrow time from the future, you'll need to stay within the limits of the time you have available.

What If Your Plan Seems Impossible?

Sometimes it seems that there is no mix of tactics and tools that will fit within your time and money budget and still bring you the number of prospects and sales conversations you need. Even when you choose tactics that will help you make contact with large numbers of people, the numbers may not add up. The higher the number of prospects you need, the more likely this is to occur.

If you encounter this situation while creating your plan, it may indicate that you need to revise some of your assumptions about your business. Your first thought might be to reduce your revenue goal, but that may not be necessary. Instead, consider whether your rates or prices should be higher. Could you pursue a target market that would result in a higher average sale? Should your business mix contain a different set of products and services or different proportions? Or do you need to find a way to spend more time or money on marketing than you previously thought?

Try changing any of these other elements of your plan first, and only reduce your revenue goal as a last resort. Even a small reduction in the total number of prospects needed can turn a seemingly impossible plan into an effective one.

From Your Model Month to a Six-Month Plan

When you have a mix of tactics and tools that works for your model month, how do you turn this into a six-month plan? The easy answer is – you duplicate it. In fact, that's not far from the truth. If you have already been actively marketing, you may have many leads and promotional opportunities already in the pipeline. If this is the case, you can turn your model month into Month 1 of your plan just by filling in the specifics of which networking group, speaking engagement, or article you plan to include in that month. "Attend networking meeting" will become "go to Breakfast Forum," and "present to group" becomes "speak to Business Alliance."

If you are just beginning your marketing and don't have all your groundwork in place yet, you will need to substitute some "getting-started" tactics or tools for some of your model month choices. For example, if your model month plan shows "warm calls to contacts" and you have no warm contacts to call, your Month 1 plan might substitute networking, cold calls, or referral-building in order to build up your warm call list for later months. Or, if your model month plan says "speak to group" and you have no presentations lined up, your Month 1 plan could substitute extra time spent on finding "speaking venues." See page 62 for an example of a Month 1 plan (July 2015).

Using this substitution method, your Month 1 plan will not yet have the payoff in prospects and presentations that your model month plan shows, but you will be building toward achieving that payoff in later months.

To turn your Month 1 plan into plans for Months 2-6, replace any getting-started activities with the original tactics you planned for your model month. Add specifics wherever possible, such as where you plan to network, speak, write, etc. Then add the tools you plan to create each month. These will change as you complete one tool and move on to the next. See page 63 for an example of a Month 2 plan (August 2015).

Each month's plan can use the same tactics over and over while just varying the tools. Or, you can decide to introduce new tactics as your plan progresses. But keep in mind that it's a good idea to use a set of tactics consistently for at least three months before deciding to switch. You need to give your tactics some time to produce results before you decide whether or not they are working.

Marketing Plan for the Month of _____

Revenue goal			
Sales goal		Marketing strategies	% of time
Prospects needed			
Conversations needed			
Hours available			
Money available			

Marketing tactics	How often How many	Hrs	$$	Pros-pects	Sales convs
Subtotals					
Marketing tools	By when	Hrs	$$		
Subtotals					
Grand total					

An Excel version of this worksheet is available in the "Free Resources" section of www.getclientsnow.com.

Revenue goal – Total annual revenue desired from your completed Business Mix Worksheet *divided by* 12.

Sales goal – Number of sales needed per month from your completed Marketing Goals Worksheet.

Prospects needed – Number of prospects needed per month from your completed Marketing Goals Worksheet. If you completed more than one Marketing Goals Worksheet because you have different lines of business, add together the total number of prospects needed from all worksheets.

Conversations needed – Number of sales conversations needed per month from your completed Marketing Goals Worksheet. If you completed more than one

Marketing Goals Worksheet because you have different lines of business, add together the total number of conversations needed from all worksheets.

Hours available – Hours available per prospect from your completed Marketing Hours Worksheet.

Money available – Money available per prospect from your completed Marketing Money Worksheet.

Marketing strategies – Strategies shown on your completed Marketing Strategy Pie worksheet.

Percent of time – Percent of time for each strategy shown on your completed Marketing Strategy Pie worksheet.

Marketing tactics – Your chosen tactics for this month, as described above.

How often/How many - Number of times you will employ this tactic and/or quantity you will generate, e.g., "five personal letters each week."

Hrs – Total hours per month needed to employ this tactic or create this tool.

$$ – Total cost expected this month to employ this tactic or create this tool.

Prospects – Number of prospects you estimate this tactic will generate.

Sales convs – Number of sales conversations you estimate this tactic will generate.

Marketing tools – Tools you plan to work on creating this month.

By when – The date by which you plan to have this tool completed.

Grand total – If greater than the hours or money you have available, or less than the number of prospects or presentations needed, *revisit your assumptions!*

Marketing Plan for the Month of Model Month

Revenue goal	$6000			
Sales goal	2	**Marketing strategies**		**% of time**
Prospects needed	60	Direct Contact & Follow-Up		45
Conversations needed	6	Networking & Referral Building		40
Hours available	40	Public Speaking		10
Money available	$300	Writing & Publicity		5

Marketing tactics	How often How many	Hrs	$$	Pros-pects	Sales convs
Warm calls to contacts	10/wk = 40	10	n/a	20	2
Send ezine to mailing list	1/mo; 1,000 subscribers	1	30	10	1
Attend networking meeting	1/mo	3	20	4	
Meet new referral partners	2/mo	3	20	4	
Contact old referral partners	4/mo	2	n/a	6	1
Speak to group & follow up	1/mo	6	10	10	2
Post to social media	3/wk	1	n/a	6	
Subtotals		26	80	60	6
Marketing tools	**By when**	**Hrs**	**$$**		
Monthly marketing project		7	100		
Handouts for speaking		2	10		
Speaking venues		2	n/a		
Article for ezine		3	n/a		
Subtotals		14	110		
Grand total		40	190	60	6

Marketing Plan for the Month of July 2015

Revenue goal	$6000		
Sales goal	2	**Marketing strategies**	**% of time**
Prospects needed	60	Direct Contact & Follow-Up	45
Conversations needed	6	Networking & Referral-Building	40
Hours available	40	Public Speaking	10
Money available	$300	Writing & Publicity	5

Marketing tactics	How often How many	Hrs	$$	Pros-pects	Sales convs
Warm calls to contacts	10/wk = 40	10	n/a	20	2
Send ezine to mailing list	1/mo; 1000 subscribers	1	30	10	1
Attend **Breakfast Forum**	1/mo	3	20	4	
Meet new referral partners	2/mo	3	20	4	
Contact old referral partners	4/mo	2	n/a	6	1
Post to social media	3/wk	1	n/a	6	
Subtotals		20	70	50	4
Marketing tools	**By when**	**Hrs**	**$$**		
Ezine template	**7/15**	2	80		
Speaking venues **(2 groups)**	**7/31**	14	n/a		
Article for **first** ezine	**7/15**	4	n/a		
Subtotals		20	80		
Grand total		40	150	50	4

Marketing Plan for the Month of August 2015

Revenue goal	$6000		
Sales goal	2	**Marketing strategies**	**% of time**
Prospects needed	60	Direct Contact & Follow-Up	45
Conversations needed	6	Networking & Referral-Building	40
Hours available	40	Public Speaking	10
Money available	$300	Writing & Publicity	5

Marketing tactics	How often How many	Hrs	$$	Pros- pects	Sales convs
Warm calls to contacts	10/wk = 40	10	n/a	20	2
Send ezine to mailing list	1/mo; 1000 subscribers	1	30	10	1
Attend **Breakfast Forum**	1/mo	3	20	4	
Meet new referral partners	2/mo	3	20	4	
Contact old referral partners	4/mo	2	n/a	6	1
Speak to **Business Alliance** & follow up	1/mo	6	10	10	2
Post to social media	3/wk	1	n/a	6	
Subtotals		26	80	60	6
Marketing tools	**By when**	**Hrs**	**$$**		
Contact mgmt system	**8/15**	7	150		
Handouts for speaking	**8/21**	2	10		
Speaking venues **(2 groups)**	**8/31**	2	n/a		
Article for ezine	**8/15**	3	n/a		
Subtotals		14	160		
Grand total		40	240	60	6

Your Marketing Plan for the Month of _____

Revenue goal			
Sales goal		Marketing strategies	% of time
Prospects needed			
Conversations needed			
Hours available			
Money available			

Marketing tactics	How often How many	Hrs	$$	Pros-pects	Sales convs
Subtotals					
Marketing tools	By when	Hrs	$$		
Subtotals					
Grand total					

WHAT DO YOU NEED TO BE SUCCESSFUL?

There is no point at which you can say,
"Well, I'm successful now. I might as well take a nap."
– CARRIE FISHER

Congratulations! You've created a customized six-month marketing plan for your business. Here are a few final tips to make your plan more powerful and effective.

Focus

Target Market – The narrower you make your target market, the easier your marketing will be. The only practical reason for a one-person business not to have a narrow target market is if one market can't give you enough business. There are other more personal reasons not to be so narrowly focused, but don't make the mistake of thinking that multiple markets are the best way to grow your business. More penetration in a single market is usually more effective.

Services Offered – As a one-person business, you already have at least three hats to wear. You must *do* the business, *market* the business, and *manage* the business at the same time. If you have more than one line of business, do you really need to be marketing them all at the same time? Marketing multiple product or service lines simultaneously can overwhelm you and confuse your market. If you want to have multiple lines because you like the variety or wish to broaden your range, try limiting yourself to marketing only three lines of business at any one time.

Tracking Results – You need to know if your marketing plan is working, so be sure to keep track. Are you getting your target number of prospects and sales conversations each month? How many of them are turning into sales? If you aren't getting the results you want, don't change the plan until you're sure you are actually working it. In other words, are you making the number of calls you said, or spending the allotted time on networking?

The only way to really know is to keep track of what you're doing, and how much time and money you're spending. If you *are* working the plan (and you've given it three months to pay off) but you're not getting the results you expected, go back to "The Universal Marketing Cycle" on page 23 and re-diagnose where you're stuck. Then revise your plan accordingly.

Expertise

If you don't know how to do something yourself or don't have the time, find an expert! **Consultants** will give you specialized advice or manage projects for you. **Coaches** will help you strategize, prioritize, learn new skills and attitudes, and keep on track. **Virtual assistants** will handle marketing tasks like researching speaking venues or sending out your ezine. **Classes and workshops** will teach you valuable information and skills. **Mentors, mastermind groups, and action groups** will give you collegial support. **Books, audios, videos, newsletters**, and **magazines** will give you new ideas and how-to's.

To receive monthly marketing tips by email, subscribe to the Get Clients Now!™ E-Letter at **www.getclientsnow.com/gcn-eletter/**. To get answers to your personal questions about marketing or find an action group for peer support, join the Get Clients Now! Online Reader Community at **www.getclientsnow.com/reader-community/**. There's no charge for either of these resources.

There's lots of help out there; just ask. Asking for help is not cheating. It's how anything important ever gets done.

Commitment

Don't give up before you've tried! Marketing plans rarely work right away – it's consistency plus persistence that really pays off. Make a commitment to work your plan for three months, no matter what. Keep track of your efforts and results. Then if things aren't working as well as you'd like, you'll know exactly where the weak points are, and how best to fix them.

You can do this!

ABOUT THE AUTHOR

C.J. Hayden, MCC, CPCC, is the best-selling author of *Get Clients Now!™*, *Get Hired Now!™*, *The One-Person Marketing Plan™ Workbook*, *50 Ways Coaches Can Change the World*, and over four hundred articles. C.J. is a business coach, trainer, and speaker who helps entrepreneurs get clients, get strategic, and get things done. Her company, Wings for Business, has been serving self-employed professionals, solopreneurs, and service business owners since 1992.

A popular speaker and workshop leader, C.J. has presented hundreds of programs on marketing, entrepreneurship, and overcoming barriers to success. She has taught marketing for John F. Kennedy University, Mills College, the U.S. Small Business Administration, and SCORE. Her articles have been published internationally in *Home Business*, *Selling Power*, and *Choice: The Magazine of Professional Coaching*. She contributes regularly to dozens of websites and ezines, including RainToday, EyesOnSales, SalesDog, and About.com.

C.J. holds the credentials Master Certified Coach from the International Coach Federation, and Certified Professional Co-Active Coach from the Coaches Training Institute. She has completed advanced coach training with the Arbinger Institute and is a member of the Arbinger Coaches Network.

C.J. has been featured in *Investor's Business Daily*, *Home Office Computing*, *Costco Connection*, and numerous books. She has been widely profiled internationally by newspapers, radio, and TV.

For more help with sales and marketing, plus many <u>free</u> resources, visit C.J.'s website www.getclientsnow.com

29756788R00043

Made in the USA
San Bernardino, CA
27 January 2016